'Have we given up trying to gain full employment? If not, what should we be trying to do about it?' These are the fundamental questions that James Meade poses, and attempts to answer in this short but timely book. As the issue of full employment moves once again to the centre of the political debate, Professor Meade draws our attention to a number of economic and financial factors which are neglected in the current debate, and suggests a novel package of changes which could be used to tackle the full-employment problem.

He condemns the neglect of macroeconomic analysis in designing full-employment policies, and asserts that the money value of total domestic production rather than the price level should be the object of a combined fiscal–monetary policy, which itself should focus on low interest rates rather than low tax rates. He argues that to achieve full employment without unacceptable inflation or poverty would require radical reforms such as labour–capital partnerships, low real wage rates offset by a universal tax-free social benefit, the abolition of national insurance contributions, and highly progressive rates of taxation of income and wealth for budget surpluses to redeem national debt.

University of Cambridge
Department of Applied Economics

Occasional paper 61

Full Employment Regained?
An Agathotopian Dream

DAE Occasional papers

Earlier titles in this series and in the DAE Papers in Industrial Relations and Labour series may be obtained from:
The Publications Secretary, Department of Applied Economics, Sidgwick Avenue, Cambridge CB3 9DE

* The Island of Agathotopia claims to be a Good Place to live in, unlike the Island of Utopia which claims to be Perfect. For a fuller discussion of Agathotopian Society see *Liberty, Equality and Efficiency* by J. E. Meade (Macmillan, 1993) and the same author's two pamphlets *Fifteen Propositions* (Employment Policy Institute, 1993) and *Full Employment without Inflation* (Employment Policy Institute and Social Market Foundation, 1994).

Full Employment Regained?

An Agathotopian Dream⋆

J. E. Meade

CAMBRIDGE
UNIVERSITY PRESS

HD
5701.5
M433
1995

Published by the Press Syndicate of the University of Cambridge
The Pitt Building, Trumpington Street, Cambridge CB2 1RP
40 West 20th Street, New York, NY 10011-4211, USA
10 Stamford Road, Oakleigh, Melbourne 3166, Australia

First published 1995

Printed in Great Britain at the University Press, Cambridge

A catalogue record for this book is available from the British Library

Library of Congress cataloguing in publication data

Meade, J. E. (James Edward), 1907–
   Full employment regained? : an Agathotopian dream / J.E. Meade.
      p.   cm. – (DAE occasional papers : 61)
   Includes bibliographical references and index.
   ISBN 0 521 55327 X (hc). – ISBN 0 521 55697 X (pb)
   1. Full employment policies. 2. Employment (Economic theory)
3. Meade, J. E. (James Edward) 1907–   . I. Title. II. Series:
Occasional papers (University of Cambridge. Dept of Applied
Economics) : 61.
   HD5701.5.M4 1995   339.5–dc20   95-17901   CIP

ISBN 0 521 55327 X hardback
ISBN 0 521 55697 X paperback

SE

Contents

Foreword

The temptation, in introducing this essay, is to dwell on the author and not the ideas. After all, James Meade was already a player in the days when Pigou and Keynes were cast as opponents in a vital intellectual struggle over the future of economics and, very likely, the economy itself. It is thus fascinating that, in the light of the ideas that circulate as hard currency in macroeconomics today, Pigou and Keynes look almost alike. Meade, for all his eminence, is thoughtfully and deliberately a throwback to those days. Herodotus may have been right to insist that we never step into the same river twice; but he was not thinking of the current that runs from Pigou and Keynes to James Meade.

This essay is about the macroeconomics of full employment (with one important digression to be mentioned later). These days it is fashionable to talk about 'job creation' and the conditions that favour it, as if all that mattered were the spirit of enterprise. That matters a lot, but probably more for the standard of living than for the volume of employment. Many newly-created jobs must displace old jobs, either directly, because a new product competes with an old one, or indirectly, because all goods and services compete for room in buyers' budgets. (Of course, the job displaced may be in another country, but Meade is mostly concerned about a closed economy, except in Chapter 5.) Everyday talk does not distinguish between 'gross' job creation and 'net' job creation.

Aggregate employment depends on the volume of aggregate expenditure and on the prices and wages that are charged in markets. Complications arise because the volume of spending depends on prices and wages, and prices and wages may depend on aggregate spending. This is a book about policy, so the first chapter after the Introduction is about demand management: the actions of governments and central banks have an influence on the volume of spending, though ministers and central-bank governors would sometimes rather not remind you of that. But it is one of the central themes of macroeconomics and Meade tackles it directly.

His preference is for public policy to take aggregate nominal spending as its proximate target. The main advantage of this choice is that a clear and credible commitment to an explicit figure would exhibit to those who make price and wage decisions that the cost of an inflationary bias in their decisions will be real contraction. Other targets – money supply, exchange rate, etc. – may have the same ultimate consequence, but less transparently.

Of course, meeting a target for nominal aggregate expenditure is not easy. In principle, it requires an understanding of the macroeconomic machinery that no one has or is likely to have, in view of the fact that economic institutions and behaviour are forever changing (sometimes in response to the policy regime itself). But that problem will always be with us. There are targets that may be easier to achieve, like one or another money supply number; but then the problem is just transferred to the tenuousness of the connection between money supply and any genuine goal of policy.

Meade is perfectly aware that successful targeting of nominal aggregate spending necessitates a unified, or at least very well coordinated, control of monetary and fiscal policy. It is hard to see how this fits with the modern preference for an independent central bank to serve as a curb on the notoriously inflationary habits of the common people. One can only suppose that the Agathotopians have got beyond this sort of schizophrenia. It would be interesting to apply the new discipline of 'political economy' to see just what might be made politically feasible in Agathotopia. As befits the last of the great utilitarians, Meade tends to be optimistic about the possibility of changing attitudes by doses of rational argument.

It would not be very Agathotopic if commitment to a reasonable level of aggregate spending were met with wage and price increases large enough to convert it into a situation of high unemployment and low real income. So Meade is forced to consider ways of inducing better behaviour from setters of wages and prices. This is a harder problem than demand management because every market is a little different from every other. No one wants the government interfering in those micro-level decisions. The usual compromise is to imagine institutional changes that might be expected to allow markets to work properly while leaning against any tendency toward an inflationary bias. That is what Meade does too.

The most striking suggestion in Chapter 3 is what he calls Discriminating Labour–Capital Partnerships. I shall leave the details to the text and only say that these are Meade's variation on the profit-sharing arrangements proposed some years ago by Martin Weitzman and on the Japanese custom of paying a substantial fraction of the compensation of workers in the form of an annual revenue-related or profit-related bonus. Meade is explicit about the 'discriminating' character of his proposal: not all workers would be treated alike. This is another place where a little political economy would be interesting. Agathotopians, after all, are merely reasonable, not saint-like. What are the internal dynamics that the spread of Discriminating Labour–Capital Partnerships would call into being? How would they turn out to behave in practice, once established?

It is characteristic of James Meade that he will not relegate the aggregative and distributional consequences of his scheme to different boxes. His primary goal is the achievement of full employment – meaning an unemployment rate of 2–3 per cent – without unacceptable inflation. He suspects that so much employment can only be achieved with fairly low real wages and a correspondingly high return to the owners of wealth, given the technology and capital stock of today and the near future. But he is unwilling to see full employment achieved at the cost of widening the gap between rich and poor. So he mulls over a number of redistributive policies. These include abolishing payroll taxes on employers and employees, making income tax more progressive, raising a larger share of revenue from pollution taxes, instituting an age-related 'Citizen's Income' or what used to be called a social dividend, moving from income taxation toward a general expenditure tax, and imposing a stiff tax on large holdings of wealth.

It cannot be said that the transition to Agathotopia would be uneventful on the political front. On the other hand, if the purpose of all this redistribution were only to offset the worsening of inequality brought about by the achievement of full employment, the necessary changes might be small, though still radical.

I have the impression that, with the bit firmly between his teeth, Meade is thinking of getting rid of a little more inequality than just that.

It has become more and more unfashionable for an economist to advocate a particular vision of the social good, as

Meade does in this little book. One reason is that economists like to think of themselves as detached scientists. Another is that some such visions are best promoted *sub rosa*. I prefer James Meade's forthright and undeceptive approach. It would be too bad if this style were to disappear. Economics and the world would lose something immensely valuable.

Robert M. Solow

Preface

I embarked on the writing of this Occasional Paper because of the neglect of macroeconomic analysis in the present lively discussions about Full-Employment policies. A strong case can be made out against excessive reliance on simple macroeconomic models for the determination of basic fiscal and monetary policies (see Simpson, 1994). But it would be disastrous in the design of such policies to neglect entirely the implications of simplified models of possible relationships between the main social-accounting variables such as the Level and Distribution of the National Income; the General Price and Wage Levels and their Rates of Inflation; the General Levels of Output, Employment, Consumption and Investment; the Budgetary Balance between Revenue and Expenditures; the International Balance of Payments; and so on.

Accordingly, the three central chapters of this book are concerned with the design of policies and institutions to control (i) the total money demand for goods and services, (ii) the setting of the general level of money prices and costs, and (iii) any consequential adverse effects on the distribution of the national income between the rich and the poor and between earned and unearned incomes. The relationships between institutions and policies designed for these three purposes are very complex; but as an old Keynesian I believe that to find an appropriate structure for these policies and institutions is a necessary condition for a successful Full-Employment policy.

The basic problem may be put in the following way. Optimists in the present debate define Full Employment as a state of affairs in which the true rate of unemployment of those who wish to work is reduced to as low a figure as 2½ or 3 per cent. Can one design a demand-management control which provides a steady market for the total output of goods and services of such a Fully-Employed economy without leading to an excessive inflationary upward pull on the prices of goods and services? Can one simultaneously devise ways of avoiding money wage claims which would cause an excessive inflationary upward push on producers' costs? What does one do if these controls lead to a totally unacceptable distribution of income between rich and poor and/or between profits and wages?

The more I thought about these matters the wider appeared to be the spread of macroeconomic relationships which were relevant to an acceptable solution of the Full-Employment problem. Indeed, I ended up producing a conglomerate of practically every reform of macro-economic policy that I have ever advocated over my 63 years as a working economist. The result suggests the need for a rather startlingly radical reform of our present economic and financial procedures.

In their general approach to the problem of Full Employment the great majority of politicians and other interested persons tend to neglect the macroeconomic issues. They concentrate on other measures such as education and training of labour and investment in modern efficient capital equipment in order to cut the costs and improve the quality of production. These reforms are of extreme importance. But they are concerned basically with raising the output per head of those who are in employment rather than about the number of heads that will find suitable employment. It is the general macroeconomic background which will determine whether a rise in output per head will lead to an unchanged output with a reduction in the number of workers employed, or to a higher output with the same number employed, or to a much higher output with a larger number employed. There is often a strange general tendency to assume that the third of these outcomes will automatically materialise without any very profound analysis of the reason why, together with a rather superficial reminder that one will need to prevent an excessive inflation of money prices.

The question arises whether Full Employment could be attained in conditions of unbridled competitive free-enterprise with everyone making the most money they can with little regard for the unsuccessful. It would certainly require very stringent controls over rates of pay to prevent a runaway inflation. With effective wage control Full Employment in otherwise fully competitive conditions would probably have two consequences.

First, it could lead to a high level and rate of growth of total output. The maintenance of a rate of growth of gross domestic product (GDP) at an annually compounded rate of 3 per cent per annum would result in the level of total output rising in the following way:

Year	1995	2005	2015	2025
GDP	100	134	181	242

Some rise in total output may be very desirable for some purposes. But in present society there is already great congestion, a high level of pollution, and an excessive strain on natural resources. These strains will be increased by more than one third in a decade from now.

Second, the analysis in this paper suggests that Full Employment in present fully competitive conditions would probably result in an extremely unequal distribution of income, with the wealthiest and most highly qualified citizens at the top of the pile enjoying extremely high incomes while those at the bottom of the pile would have to accept very low rates of pay in order to find employment. I should regard such an outcome as intolerable. To deal with it would require more emphasis on the distribution of income and less on the level and rate of growth of total output.

One remedy would be to take the productivity benefits of increased output per unit of work in the form of shorter hours of work. This would enable the unemployed to be absorbed into the work force without any increase in the total amount of work done. In brief, the time has come to encourage a leisure economy, a problem which raises many issues which are not discussed in this paper. But a move in this direction would both curb excessive output and also decrease inequalities between the employed and the unemployed.

But the necessary direct attack on inequalities, which is a major concern of this paper, would involve far-reaching radical reforms of present policies and institutions expressly designed for this more egalitarian purpose. It is very possible that my proposals for putting greater emphasis on a more equitable distribution of income would have disincentive effects on the growth of total output; but in my view we would be wise to start now gradually preparing the way for a more leisured and compassionate society, even at the cost of a somewhat lower rate of growth of total output. My attitude to Full-Employment policies has been much affected by the difficult tasks of promoting an appropriate change in the political assessment of what constitutes a good society.

Chapter 1

▲

Introduction

In the years immediately after the Second World War the great aim of economic thought and policy was to achieve and maintain a state of Full Employment. The mood was much affected by memories of the Great Depression of the pre-war decade and by the promotion of Keynesian ideas. More recently, the emphasis of economic policy has turned onto the control of a threatening runaway inflation, a control which has been exercised at the expense of the recurrence of mass unemployment and of an increasing inequality between the incomes of the rich and the poor. Now once again Full Employment is seriously considered as a primary aim of policy. Can it be regained without serious inflation and increasing inequality?

To answer this question requires consideration of a whole package of separate but very closely related economic and financial policies. This book describes a much simplified macroeconomic model of relevant interactions between the various policies. These macroeconomic policies constitute an essential part of the problem of achieving and maintaining Full Employment, but the simple model presented in this paper neglects a number of the conditions which are essential for the final solution of the problem.

In the first place, the model presented in this paper is basically restricted to the relationships in a closed economy. In the present condition of a global world economy it may seem absurd to write anything substantial on a single country's domestic economic arrangements without giving the same degree of attention to the implications for that country's external economic and financial relations with the rest of the world. But we may refer to the great example of Keynes's revolutionary book *The General Theory* which concentrated on the problems in a closed economy, leaving much subsequent discussion and research to determine their international implications. Chapter 5 of this book does, however, very briefly sketch the direction in which the international implications of the present proposals would need to be considered.

In the second place, there would be no chance of implementing the proposed package of domestic economic reforms in the absence of a political consensus as to their desirability. In particular, society would need to appreciate them as a move in the direction of building a decent, equitable community of citizens rather than of concentrating on the freedom of the individual citizen to make the best killing that he or she can make, with the devil taking the unsuccessful.

Such a cultural change would certainly take some time; but the position is not necessarily hopeless. If political leaders could advocate moderate reforms in the desired direction the man or woman in the street may begin to listen. There may well be positive feedback between economic arrangements and the culture of society. As the economic reforms progress the attitudes of society may become more favourable to change and as the cultural attitude improves so the economic reforms may be made more radical.

There are two aspects of economic reform which play prominent roles in present discussions about possible Full-Employment policies. The first concerns the qualifications and adaptability of the UK's labour force and the second concerns the availability of efficient modern capital equipment and infrastructure.

Basic changes designed to improve the productivity, skills, adaptability and general qualifications of the working citizens are needed in the realms of training, education, health, caring for the children of working mothers, etc. They are of extreme importance, should be pursued with vigour, and are in no way incompatible with the macro-economic proposals which are considered in greater detail in this book.

There are, alas, at present many politicians and other influential persons who in designing present fashionable Full-Employment policies argue as if these supply-side quality reforms were alone of importance in the labour market. They put relatively little stress on the problems of maintaining moderation in wage claims – to the astonishment of some economists who, like the present author, consider that the supply *price* set for a good or service is as vital a factor as its *quality* in determining its saleability.

Basic changes are needed also in business attitudes, trade and industry policies, and in monetary and fiscal arrangements to ensure sufficient investment in effective capital equipment and the provision of an adequate and appropriate infrastructure.

I regard suitable widespread reforms in these two fields of supply of labour and of capital as of the greatest importance. But they are not studied in the present book which is concerned with a quite different set of economic and financial reforms, constituting an essential but sadly neglected necessary condition for achieving and maintaining Full Employment.

This neglected area of problems is concerned with the network of interrelationships between certain macro-economic variables such as the general level of money prices, the rate of interest, the rate of tax, the level of government expenditures, the budget deficit or surplus, and so on. An analysis of these interrelationships leads to proposals for a number of economic and financial control policies as being necessary to maintain Full Employment without an excessive inflation or an unacceptably unequal distribution of income and wealth. This analysis is based on a very greatly simplified and rather mechanical macroeconomic model which pays little attention to a number of important issues concerning expectations, incentives and administrative difficulties.

Nevertheless, in my opinion, there still remains a coherent, though limited, set of control problems. The positive propositions which result from this study may be summarised as follows:

(1) that Full Employment depends upon two main conditions: first, that there are proper demand-management arrangements to ensure an adequate and stable level of money expenditures on goods and services and thus to enable the output of a Fully-Employed economy to find a steady and reliable market; and, second, that the workers who seek employment in a free-enterprise economy, given their skills and qualifications, offer their services at a low enough real price for competing employers to employ them;

(2) that this price of labour at the low end of the income scale would in a free market almost certainly be so low as to present a socially undesirable distribution of income;

(3) that, combined with the seller's market for labour implied by an unemployment rate of 2 to 3 per cent, this relatively low wage would almost certainly lead to claims for wage increases on a scale which threatened an explosive inflation;

(4) that the basic economic problems of the future will be concerned with the distribution of the national income rather than with the production of an evergrowing output of goods and services;

(5) that Full Employment may thus increasingly become a question of part-time working with a greater use of leisure; and

(6) that Full Employment with a fair distribution of a high national income and with employment being relatively low-paid and increasingly part-time will necessitate very great changes in many of our existing economic and financial institutions and policies, the discussion of which constitutes the subject matter of the rest of this book.

Chapter 2

▲

Demand Management

We may define 'Demand Management' as governmental control over the total money value of expenditures on domestically produced goods and services. This total may usefully be divided into three categories:

(1) expenditure by the government itself on goods and services, which excludes budgetary expenditures on transfers of money to the private sector such as interest payments on the national debt or monetary social welfare benefits;

(2) expenditures by individuals or by corporate bodies in the private sector on goods and services for capital investment purposes; and

(3) expenditures made by the private sector for consumption purposes.

Much expenditure in category (1) is, of course, relevant for employment purposes, such as expenditures on education, health, and social infrastructure etc. The government can itself directly control such expenditures. For this reason, this chapter is confined to government actions taken to influence private-sector expenditures in categories (2) and (3) indirectly by means of monetary and fiscal policies of various kinds.

The primary purpose of demand management is to maintain a high and steady market for goods and services, that is to say, to control the sum total of categories (1), (2) and (3) at a high enough level to absorb the total output of goods and services which can be produced in conditions of Full Employment and to prevent temporary fluctuations in that level of total expenditures.

But there is a second very important purpose, namely to control the split of the sum total of expenditures between expenditures on goods and services for capital investment and those for immediate consumption. This split is of very great importance for the future maintenance of Full Employment, since the greater the capital capacity in the economy, the higher will be the real demand for labour at any given real rate of pay. The consideration of the effects of different financial policies on capital investment expenditures (in category 2) and on consumption expenditures (in category 3) will thus form an important role in the present chapter.

We start then with a discussion of the first of these two ideas, namely the control of the total of all three categories of expenditures on domestic products. This idea of total Demand Management originated from the pre-war work of

Keynes, who regarded the purpose of raising or lowering general incentives to spend money on domestically produced goods and services as an indirect means of maintaining the employment of labour at a high and stable level.

But there have always been those who feared that, even in conditions of heavy unemployment, the policy of deliberately planning increased monetary expenditures would probably lead to inflation rather than to increased employment. In pre-war Keynesian analysis there had been relatively little reference to such inflationary dangers. So long as there were substantial unemployed resources of men and machines available to be brought into use it was assumed that one could expect increased demand to lead to increased output and employment. Inflation would become the greater danger when no more goods and services could be produced for sale; and indeed there had been very considerable evidence that expansion of output and employment was the primary effect of increased demand in the pre-war highly depressed economy.

For two decades or so after the war it seemed that there was validity in the Keynesian prescription for maintaining demand at a Full-Employment level and that this did not involve any intolerable inflationary pressure.

The immediate post-war situation was a period of confident hope for the future which started from a stable cost of living due to wartime price controls and food subsidies and with a patriotic wartime habit of great restraint in wage demands. This involved more or less complete money illusion – bargains being struck on the assumption that the real value of money would not be much changed. But with Full Employment workers began to realise their bargaining power. Money wage rates and prices began to rise. The cost of living thus rose. Attempts to meet the rise in the cost of living by domestic wage increases set in motion an explosive inflation. Money illusion disappeared. People demanded rises in pay to offset future expected rises in the cost of living as well as to exercise bargaining power to obtain a net real increase in standards of living.

In 1973–4, the danger of explosive price inflation was much increased by a big upward jolt in the cost of imported oil and so in the price of all oil-using goods and services. This intensified the demand for higher rates of pay to offset the rise in the cost of living. But in fact the rise in the cost of an important raw material represented an increase in the real costs of domestic products equivalent to a fall in productivity. The avoidance of explosive inflation demanded the acceptance of the rise in the cost of living without any pressure for offsetting increases in rates of pay.

Threats of explosive inflation were met by financial restrictions leading to unemployment – first in fits and starts with Stop–Go. Prices and incomes policies were then tried but abandoned, possibly too readily. Clearly they were extremely difficult to arrange and very unpopular with trade unions and businesses. In any case, for reasons to be explained later, they alone are insufficient to solve the basic problem. Finally came the Thatcherite insistence on a greatly reduced and low rate of inflation as the basic financial objective, to be achieved by accepting a long and apparently endless period of restrictive financial policy and mass unemployment. The wheel had turned full-circle, with financial policy's main aim becoming a low rate of inflation instead of a high level of employment and with general depression being treated once again as in pre-Keynesian days as a cyclical Act of God.

So the basic question arises of how to get Full Employment without a high rate of inflation and above all without explosive inflation. What for this purpose should be the financial policy objective? The sorry story of the monetarist experiments may clear the ground for the restatement of a feasible financial objective.

With the abandonment of full employment, the control of inflation became the primary objective of monetary policy. For this purpose the adjustment of the stock of money (M) was at first chosen as the means of controlling the general level of money prices (P) of goods and services; and the market was left to determine any resulting levels of output and employment.

The idea that increasing the stock of money – for example by issuing more bank notes or increasing the supply of bank deposits – may be a reliable method of raising *pro rata* the general level of money prices is based on the simple fact that the amount of money in existence (M) multiplied by the frequency or velocity (V) with which each unit of M passes from buyer to seller of goods and services will measure the level of total money expenditure on goods and services. At the same time that the buyer spends £1 in the purchase of the goods the seller receives an addition of £1 to his or her receipts from sales, so that MV measures not only the total of money expenditures by customers but also the total receipts of producers.

But the total receipts of producers depend upon the quantity of goods and services sold (Q) multiplied by the price of these goods and services (P). Thus the total expenditure on the purchase of goods and services equals the total receipts from the sale of these goods and services, or $MV = PQ$.

It is clear from this that controlling M at a stable value will be an effective way of stabilising P only if V and Q remain at unchanged stable values. Otherwise, there could be large changes in P even though M was kept constant.

In fact there are many ways in which combinations of changes in V, P and Q can occur even if M is held constant. One example must suffice. Even with MV constant there could be a marked fall in Q offset by a marked rise in P. This is simply a description of the well-known phenomenon of Stagflation, an inflation of price being accompanied by a deflation of output and an increase in unemployment.

But the most ludicrous aspect of the whole calamitous

history of using M as a means of controlling P remains to be described. In present conditions it is extremely difficult, for two reasons, to define what does and what does not constitute the stock of money (M) which one should use for stabilising purposes. First, many institutions other than the familiar commercial banks (for example, building societies) can provide readily transferable liabilities which for many purposes it is difficult to distinguish from bank deposits; and bank deposits themselves are no longer sharply divided into non-interest bearing balances transferable at sight and interest-bearing liabilities cashable only after giving due notice. In the second place, credit cards and other electronic devices for the transfer of funds provide in effect instant overdraft facilities with often ill-defined limits and conditions; and there seems to be no end to new electronic devices for transferring purchasing power from one account to another. How then to add together these possibilities to form a single stock of money (M) existing at any moment of time? During the period of the monetarist regime attempts were made to 'add' together in various combinations stocks of 'money' held in different forms for different purposes ($M0$, $M1$, $M2$, $M3$, $M4$) and to consider which of them seemed most appropriate to use. But for this purpose, of course, one had first to decide what price level (P) one wished to stabilise – that is to say, what package of goods and services (Q) one wished to cover in the price stabilisation scheme. No agreement could be reached on which was the most suitable M to use for control purposes, with the different Ms persisting in moving at different speeds in different directions.

Eventually it was realised that, if the ultimate objective was to control some given price level (P), one might simply leave out the monetarist mumbo-jumbo and make the price level itself the primary objective of financial policy, relaxing or restricting monetary and fiscal policies directly to prevent P from straying from its planned target level. So the next step was to take a price index (P instead of M) as the objective of monetary policy. The problem then was to choose a suitable P.

A popular choice was the price of a foreign currency (e.g., the sterling–mark exchange rate). But this was to surrender the country's control over its own macroeconomic policy and accept whatever monetary inflation or deflation the German financial authorities chose for their own domestic purposes. This shrugging off on to another country of all responsibility for our domestic welfare did not work well.

If, however, a P is chosen for the purpose of controlling one's own undesirable inflationary or deflationary forces it should exclude the price effects of imported goods and services, and, for similar reasons, the price effects of indirect taxes such as VAT which are expressly designed to make certain domestic products more expensive to the domestic consumer. P should be the money price of domestically produced goods and services, i.e., the money deflator of the GDP.

Suppose that an inflation of a general price index is caused by a rise in the prices of imported goods and services. To rule that it is only the prices of domestic products that should be stabilised would involve the avoidance of a rise in rates of pay designed to offset the imported element of the rise in the cost of living. That task is difficult enough. But to rule that the general price index (including the price of imports) should be stabilised would involve an absolute reduction in domestic rates of pay and prices on a scale sufficient to offset the rise in the price of imports. This would be much more difficult. It would involve creating a sufficiently severe depression of output and employment to enforce absolute reductions of rates of pay which in fact served little or no useful purpose.

The argument is equally true of an increase in VAT which is intended to reduce real consumption. To say that the whole structure of domestic wage rates and prices must be deflated to prevent a rise in P which includes VAT is sadistic nonsense. But this is the torture to which one is committed by setting a rigid limit on the rise in the Retail Price Index. The only sensible P to choose to control domestic price-cost inflation is the money GDP deflator. But even the stabilisation of this P is an unsuitable financial objective.

One must admit that making the control of prices the

primary objective of financial policy can be amazingly effective and successful. Over the last ten years or so the rate of price inflation has been reduced from around 20 per cent to 3 or 4 per cent per annum – but at the expense of a deep and prolonged depression of output and employment.

A better approach is to employ financial policy (i.e., a combination of monetary and fiscal policies) to control the money GDP – i.e., the total level of expenditures of money on domestically produced goods and services.

The basic case for using money GDP rather than prices as the over-riding financial objective can be put very simply. Suppose there is some development in the economy which causes the start of a recession. Money wage rates and prices being sticky, though not rigid, the first and marked effect of the recession will be a fall in output and employment which will only later and gradually cause some deflation of the price level. If money GDP is successfully adopted as the policy target, any marked decline in the demand for goods and services will promptly be offset by financial policy measures to maintain the total money GDP. If the price level is the objective of financial policy, there will be an offsetting policy expansion only when and to the limited extent that unemployment has so grown as to cause a decline in the price level. The maintenance of *money* GDP has a much more rapid effect than the stabilisation of the price level on the stabilisation of employment. Thus it has much of the merit of the original Keynesian prescription to use financial policy to maintain *real* GDP – the general level of output and employment.

It is often argued that the statistical problems of calculating money GDP and its probable future movements rule it out as the basic financial target. These difficulties are much exaggerated. Much thought is being given to new methods for the improvement of national income figures with sufficient success for serious professional work to have been set in motion to construct a reliable monthly index of money GDP. Moreover, whatever objective is chosen for control by financial policy – the level of employment, the stock of money, the price level, or money GDP – a forecast of their probable future movements is what is needed for control purposes. There is always an important element of uncertainty in such forecasts and with the recent improvements in estimating movements of national income figures there is no reason why money GDP should be less effective than the available alternatives to play the part of target for financial control purposes.

There is no general deflationary implication in choosing money GDP (or *PQ*) as the main objective of financial policy. The initial target for money GDP could be set at a significantly higher level than the existing current level if it were considered desirable to give the economy an initial inflationary boost. If one believes that a moderate continuous steady inflation is desirable, the future path for money GDP could be set at a rate of growth which is high enough to cover any expected future growth in the size of the available labour force, offset by any expected growth of labour's marginal productivity, but high enough to allow for a moderate annual rate of inflation. The only deflationary aspect of the system would be that further inflation above the chosen level would lead to financial restriction and so to restriction of output and employment sufficient to restrain the excessive inflation. Indeed, there are at least two very good reasons for believing that some moderate and steady rate of price inflation may be a desirable objective.

In the first place, in a developing economy it will be necessary to allow for some movement of workers from an occupation or region which is declining to one which is growing in relative importance; and this process will be greatly eased by a fall in the rate of pay in the declining sector relatively to the rate of pay in the expanding sector. But rates of pay are set in terms of money and it is much easier to change the relative rates of real rewards by a rise in the money rates in the expanding sectors than by a reduction of money rates of pay in the declining sectors. Thus a moderate inflation of average money prices eases readjustments of the economy.

In the second place, the real cost of raising funds for capital development is equal to the money rate of interest less the rate of price inflation. A moderate rate of price inflation then allows the money rate of interest to be maintained at a higher level without increasing the real cost of capital development. There may well be technical banking difficulties in maintaining very low money rates of interest. This means that the very low real rates of interest which may be needed at times of economic recession can be achieved more easily if prices are normally rising at a moderate rate of inflation.

Even a negative real rate of interest can be achieved (and indeed in the past has been achieved) simply by the maintenance of a money rate of interest which is lower than the rate of price inflation. The use of interest rates as a means of demand management may be easier in moderately inflationary conditions.

We conclude that the objective of demand-management policies should be to keep total money expenditure on domestically produced goods and services (i.e., the money GDP) on a planned, steadily rising path. We now turn to a consideration of the means by which expenditures can be controlled so as not to diverge substantially from this target path.

These controls can be exercised through monetary and/or fiscal policies. If the money GDP strays above its target level, the Central Bank can adopt a more restrictive, monetary policy which will cause the rate of interest to rise in the capital market, thus making it more costly to raise funds to spend on new purchases. Similarly, fiscal policies may be made more restrictive, for example by raising the rate of income tax, thus leaving tax payers with smaller spendable incomes. And, *vice versa*, less restrictive monetary and fiscal policies can be adopted if money GDP falls below its target level.

These direct 'impact' effects of restrictive monetary or fiscal policies will be followed by what are called indirect 'multiplier' effects. Thus consider an 'impact' effect of a reduction of expenditures by £100m caused by a restrictive monetary or fiscal policy. This reduction of demand for goods and services will cause the incomes of the producers of the goods and services to fall by £100m. As a result of the reduction in their incomes these producers will pay less in tax and will probably cut down their savings, but for the rest (say £50m) they will have to spend less on other goods and services. This means that in turn some other producers of goods and services will face a reduction of their incomes by £50m and after paying less in tax and cutting their savings they will have to spend less (say £25m) on their purchases of goods and services, and so on in a cycle of falling expenditures until the farther repercussions become negligible. Thus, with these 'multiplier' effects added to their 'impact' effects, both a rise in the rate of interest and a rise in the rate of tax could be used effectively as a means of restraining money expenditures. Does it, therefore, make no difference which method is chosen for the control of money GDP?

There are in fact three ways in which the two methods of control differ very markedly.

In the first place, their 'impact' effects, though not their 'multiplier' effects, probably are very different. A rise in the rate of interest is more likely to lead to a reduction in borrowing for investment in capital assets and a rise in the rate of income tax is more likely to lead to a reduction in consumption expenditures.

Secondly, there is a very important distinction between the speed, frequency, and promptness with which monetary and fiscal controls can be operated. An undesirable upward or downward swing in money incomes and prices, unless it is promptly interrupted, can feed upon itself and grow as its future continuation becomes more and more confidently expected. This tells heavily in favour of the use of monetary policy as a short-term stabiliser of money GDP. A Central Bank's rate of interest can be adjusted as soon as change is judged desirable. But the rate of income tax is normally changeable only once a year and a more frequent or prompt change presents real difficulty.[1]

Thirdly, the net effects on the budget balance of a rise in the rates of interest and of a rise in the rate of tax may well

---

[1] This does not mean that fiscal policies could not be made more flexible than they are at present. Measures for altering the rates of indirect taxes such as VAT more frequently have been considered and for a short time actually used for stabilising purposes. It might also be possible to use variations in some items of government expenditures (such as the Citizen's Income discussed later in Chapter 4) as stabilisers of total expenditures.

differ. Both forms of restriction, by decreasing the total level of money GDP, will cause a reduction of tax revenue. A rise in the rate of interest will also have the effect of worsening the budgetary balance by increasing government expenditures on debt interest. On the other hand, a rise in the rate of tax will itself improve the budgetary position by increasing the revenue on the diminished total of money incomes and expenditures. The ultimate outcome will depend upon the circumstances of each particular case. But a quite probable outcome is that, while a rise in the rate of interest will worsen the budget balance, a rise in the rate of tax will improve it.

These three differences in the effects of monetary and of fiscal policies should be taken into account in determining the structure of financial controls of money GDP. Compare two sets of controls: set A has a relatively high rate of interest and a relatively low rate of tax, while set B has a relatively low rate of interest and a relatively high rate of tax, both sets being so constructed as to keep money GDP on the same target level. Given that they produce the same GDP the only relevant differences between them will be (i) that through their 'impact' effects set A will lead to a relatively high ratio of consumption to capital investment and set B to a relatively high ratio of capital investment to consumption; and (ii) that through the effect of low rates of interest in reducing the cost of servicing the national debt and of high tax rates in raising the budgetary revenue, set B will have a more favourable effect then set A on the budget balance. On both these counts, in my opinion, set B with high tax rates and low interest rates is in present circumstances preferable to set A.

If, however, through some unforeseen shock to the system a self-reinforcing unexpected boom or slump in money incomes and prices should develop, it will be necessary to take counter measures promptly. For this purpose great reliance will have to be placed on monetary policy, with a rise in interest rates to nip a boom in the bud, or *vice versa* in the case of a slump.

It is possible to draw one very important conclusion from this general discussion, namely that monetary and fiscal policies must be planned and operated as a single whole by a single financial authority. To make a Central Bank an independent agency with the basic duty of preventing excessive inflation of the price level (or preferably of money GDP), while the governmental budgetary authority has the separate duty of determining rates of tax and governmental expenditures and thus the budget balance, is to invite disaster.

To take an extreme example, consider an economy in which there are very large indirect 'multiplier' effects of any given change in expenditures due to a change in monetary or fiscal policy. Suppose that the Minister of Finance decides to raise the rate of income tax in order to eliminate a budget deficit. The rise in the rate of tax will lead to a heavy fall in total money GDP because of the large 'multiplier' effects following the direct 'impact' reduction in expenditures due to the fall in tax payers' post-tax incomes.

But the heavy fall in total money GDP will cause a heavy fall in total taxable incomes which will lead to a heavy fall in tax revenue due to the fall in the tax base. This indirect fall in tax will wipe out a lot of the original direct increase in tax revenue due to the rise in the rate of tax. It might theoretically be so great as to wipe out the whole of the original increase in revenue. The 'multiplier' effects will at least greatly reduce the net yield from the higher tax rate. The rate of tax will need to be raised still further to wipe out the whole of the original budget deficit with a further round of reduction in money GDP, taxable income, and net yield of revenue; and so on in a series of cycles of falling money GDP.

The only way to avoid this heavy undesirable fall of money GDP below its target level would have been to arrange for a reduction in the rate of interest by the Central Bank to stimulate a direct increase of money expenditures through monetary policy equal to, and simultaneous with, the 'impact' fall in money expenditures due to the original fiscal-policy increase in the rate of tax. If the Central Bank is left independent to decide if and when and how much it will lower its interest rate to offset an undesirable fall in money GDP, the demand management desire to maintain money GDP at a stable target level will in all probability be replaced by a heavy downward swing, followed by a heavy upward swing of money GDP.

The above comments on the choice between monetary and fiscal controls for purposes of demand management have been based on the assumptions that monetary policy can take the form only of changes in the rate of interest and that fiscal policy can take the form only of changes in the rate of income tax. In fact, of course, there can be a great variety of monetary and fiscal instruments of control.

This variety is particularly great and important in the case of fiscal policies. These can operate on the expenditure as well as on the revenue side of the budget, and there are many different objects and forms of government expenditure and of government revenue. A number of these varieties will be mentioned in the following chapters of this book, and in particular in connection with the distribution of income in Chapter 4. Many of these varieties of fiscal policy have no very direct relevance to demand-management problems, being designed primarily to cope with other problems. But in planning a joint combined financial strategy, the demand-management advantages or disadvantages of each element in the final plan should play an important, though not necessarily a decisive, part.

Chapter 3

▲

The Setting of Prices and Wage Rates

We turn from the demand-management problem to the problem of the price structure required for Full Employment.

If there were perfect competition in all markets in a wholly free-enterprise economy, in which demand management was completely successful in keeping total demand (i.e., money GDP) on a steady, reliable pre-planned path, the answer would be easy. Do nothing: leave free competition to clear all markets for labour and for other goods and services.

As far as the labour market is concerned, anyone who wanted a job would offer himself or herself to a suitable employer at a slightly lower wage than the present employee. This would exert a downward pressure on wage rates until one reached Full Employment without inflation.

At the same time, perfect competition among those who were saving or owned capital funds and between the entrepreneurs and managers who used the capital funds would result in attracting capital and enterprise to the

supply of the goods and services for which competing consumers offered the best price, these goods and services
being produced in the ways which cost least. The whole
system would in this well known text book manner lead to
Full Employment without excessive inflation and to using
resources in ways which were most efficient in meeting the
demands of the consumers.

The basic snag in this whole competitive process is the
possibility that it would lead to an intolerable degree of
inequality in the distribution of income and wealth. The
system, even if it were a realistic economic possibility,
would be politically unacceptable unless modified on
distributional grounds.

We may consider first the distribution of the national
income between pay for work done and the return of rents,
dividends, interest and profits on the ownership of capital
wealth. The outcome would depend on three factors: (i)
the supply of labour relative to that of capital; (ii) the extent
to which consumers' demands were for capital-intensive
rather than labour-intensive products; and (iii) the degree
to which production technologies were labour or capital
saving. If all three of these factors were high the real wage
might be miserably low and the incomes of capitalists
excessively high.

As far as the first of these three factors is concerned, it is
worth noting that a movement from mass unemployment
to Full Employment would itself be the equivalent of an

increase in the supply of labour, but that the instruments chosen for demand-management control, as argued in Chapter 2, could be designed to encourage investment in new capital goods. As far as the third of the three factors is concerned, it is probable that 'chips and robots' will continue to replace unskilled manual workers.

Even in a perfectly competitive model of the economy it would be totally wrong to neglect the differences between different types of workers. There are at present immense differences in qualifications among the working population, leading to immense differences in the salaries, wages and other forms of payment for work done. However great the improvements which may be achieved in qualifications at the lower end of the scale, substantial differences in qualifications will, for innate or other reasons, still remain. Moreover, technical changes in industry may well lead to an increase in the commercial value of highly qualified relative to less highly qualified workers, as well as leading to an increase in the profits on capital relative to the wages of labour. There is in fact already in the real world a tendency for the distribution of income to become more and more unequal.

It is hoped that this sketch of the forces which would be at work in a perfectly competitive economy may be useful in drawing attention to some of the basic forces at work in a real world in which free enterprise is allowed as much play as is possible. But it is time to drop the assumption of perfect competition.

The world is not made up of perfectly competitive atomistic units and the idea of leaving the removal of involuntary unemployment to the freedom of the market is in fact ludicrous. Differences of location, of type of product, of the commercial and engineering abilities of managers, together with economies of scale which make it unprofitable to introduce a small-scale enterprise to fill a small gap in location or type of product, mean that our world is made up of a large number of concerns each with some monopolistic elements ranging from the special locational advantage of the shop in a village in which there is not really room for two, to ICI with its huge advantage of scale and special products. Such structures mean that when demand for a concern's products goes up there is always an element of choice as to whether the concern will use this improvement to expand its output and employment at present prices and wages, or whether it will raise its prices and increase the rate of dividend and wages of its existing capitalists and workers. The clash of interest is largely between the insiders and the outsiders: for example, between the employed and the unemployed.

Experience suggests that pressure from the outsiders (the unemployed) does exert some restraining influence on the use of funds exclusively for the insiders' benefit and that if a depression becomes deep enough with the unemployment percentage high enough the existing concerns and their workers will be restrained from raising their prices at an excessive rate.

It has been suggested that a Full-Employment target for the unemployment percentage might be set at 2½ to 3 per cent. To maintain the demand for labour at this height would certainly involve a seller's market for labour, with a high search for workers by employers relative to the search for employers by workers. In such a very strong bargaining position there would be a very strong upward pressure on money wages and product prices.

Some rise of rates of pay per worker could occur without causing any inflation of money prices if the marginal cost of the workers to the employers were falling. Average labour costs will be falling, since output per head will continue to grow in a Full- Employment situation insofar as (i) supply-side quality reforms (see pages 5–6 above) are improving the productivity of workers, (ii) current investment is increasing real capital per worker, (iii) technical improvements in methods of production are raising output per worker and (iv) the increasing total output of products due to the three foregoing factors is leading to economies of scale.[2]

These increases in output per head do not necessarily increase the marginal value of the workers to the same extent. Thus, according as the technical improvements under (iii) are labour saving or capital saving, the increase

---

[2] I thank Professor Frank Hahn for emphasising the effects of increasing returns to scale on the Full-Employment problem.

in the marginal value of the workers to employers will be less than or greater than the rise in output per head. A similar consideration applies to increases in output per head due to the increased scale of production mentioned under (iv). In a free market economy it depends upon whether the increase in output per head due to the increase in scale of production is mainly due to a greater and better use of lumpy capital equipment or to the advantages of greater specialisation and division of labour among various tasks for workers.

The demand-management target rate of growth of money GDP could be planned at a high enough figure to offset any such net decreases in the marginal cost of labour to the employers plus an allowance for any steady and reliable net rate of inflation of prices that was considered to be generally desirable (see pages 22–3 above). If workers bargained for a rate of increase of pay at this restricted rate even in the seller's labour market which would be a feature of an unemployment percentage of only 2½ to 3 per cent, there would be no excessive inflationary danger. But if, as is probable, the rate of wage increases were greater than this permissible rate, there would be a danger of an explosive runaway inflation.

A simple numerical example may make clear the nature of this explosive inflationary danger. Suppose that the plan is to keep price inflation down to zero, in conditions in which the productivity of labour is rising at 2 per cent per annum and producers are setting their selling prices equal to their labour costs plus a fixed percentage write-up for a profit margin. If labour's money wage rises 2 per cent per annum there will be no increase in labour costs and thus no increase in product prices. But if money wage rates rise at 3 per cent per annum because labour aims at a 3 per cent per annum rise in its real rate of pay, labour costs and so prices would rise by 1 per cent per annum. Labour might then raise its money wage claim to 4 per cent per annum to offset the 1 per cent per annum rise in the cost of living; labour costs and so selling prices would then rise by 2 per cent per annum. If at the next round labour raised its wage claim to 5 per cent per annum in order to offset the 2 per cent rise in the cost of living, labour costs and so product prices would be raised by 3 per cent per annum. And so on in a continuous raising of money wage rates chasing a resulting continuous and unlimited rise in the cost of living.[3] The speed of the rise in the rate of inflation would itself be continuously increased if labour tried to anticipate the future rate of inflation instead of simply reacting to past changes in the rate of inflation.

[3] Ten years after the rise in real wage claim from 2 to 3 per cent per annum, an exact chase of this kind would lead to a rate of price inflation not of 10 per cent per annum but of $(1.03/1.02)''$ equal approximately to $11\frac{1}{3}$ per cent per annum. For a further discussion of an explosive inflation see Meade, 1994, p. 13.

If this sort of situation did occur, the only remedy with present institutions would be through restrictive demand-management controls to reduce the demand for labour sufficiently below the Full-Employment level to curb its bargaining power in wage settlements. This would be the function of setting a target level for money GDP.

As long as unemployment remains at a sufficiently high level to curb the bargaining power of the workers this threat of runaway inflation may not materialise. But it is very likely to occur as one approaches Full Employment. The lasting success of a Full-Employment situation probably depends upon being prepared well in advance with some solution for this most difficult Full-Employment problem ready to be applied as and when the need for it does arise.

Many elements of a solution have been discussed in the past. They should all become immediately a subject of the most serious thought and reconsideration. Increasing competition by clearing the channels of domestic and international trade; institutions to prevent monopolistic arrangements; price regulation of privatised concerns; and the setting of uninflated prices in nationalised concerns – these are all measures suitable for holding down product prices. Control of prices and wages by a Board for Prices and Incomes; legislation against trade unions' monopolistic practices; compulsory arbitration in pay bargaining disputes with the arbitrators required to accept whichever side proposes the settlement which is most likely to promote employment; and a tax on inflationary rises in rates of pay – these are all measures which have been considered in the past for the restraint of rises in rates of pay. It is not intended in this short book to examine these measures in detail. But the choice between, and the practicability of application of, these various methods of control should become once again the subject of most serious study with a determination to be ready for the most rigorous and effective application of the chosen policies.

One idea may be added to the above list. Surprisingly little attention has been paid to the effects of applying the rule of equal pay for equal work to those who provide labour but without any corresponding rule of equal return on equal machines for those who supply capital instruments of production.[4] Consider a concern which has done exceptionally well. Those who subscribed the original funds to purchase the original batch of machinery will have made a big capital gain on their shareholdings. If the company finds it profitable to expand by issuing a further batch of shares to purchase a further batch of machines, the original shareholders would feel no obligation to share their existing capital gains with the new shareholders. They

[4] For a numerical example of this important distinction see Proposition 2 in Meade, 1993a. See also the Appendix in Meade, 1994.

would issue just that limited number of shares at the new inflated price as was necessary to raise the funds for the purchase of the new batch of machines. The old capitalists maintain their exceptional capital gains; the new capitalists for providing just the same number of similar machines receive only what is necessary to attract them into the business.

Labour is treated quite differently. Pay may be exceptionally high in an exceptionally successful business. It might pay everyone to take on more labour at a rate of pay good in comparison with outside market rates of pay for such labour (e.g., the rate of unemployment benefit) but not at a rate as high as the relatively high rate enjoyed by the existing insiders. In this case, for employment to be expanded either the insiders have to agree to a reduction in their rate of pay to whatever level is necessary to make it worthwhile employing the additional workers on equal terms, or else the principle of equal pay for equal work must be abandoned. Would it not be possible to devise labour–capital partnership arrangements in which this obstacle to the expansion of the employment of labour could be removed? Existing partners would be free to take on new partners on terms which were less than those enjoyed by the existing partners but were attractive to the new partners as compared with their opportunities outside the market (e.g., unemployment benefit).

In fact, a suitably designed Discriminating Labour–Capital Partnership[5] could make an important contribution to the solution of the Full-Employment problem.

The capital resources employed in such a partnership are financed by the issue of Capital Share Certificates to those who provide the necessary funds, these corresponding to the ordinary shares of a normal capitalist company.

The distinctive feature of a Labour–Capital Partnership is that the working partners are not paid at a fixed wage rate but by the issue to them of an appropriate number of Labour Share Certificates, on which exactly the same dividend is paid as on the Capital Share Certificates. This has the important result that any decision taken by the management (representing both Capital and Worker Partners) which increases the profit of the enterprise and so the rate of dividend payable on all share certificates would accrue in equal proportion to both Labour and Capital Partners.

There is, however, one important distinction between Capital and Labour Share Certificates. The former will continue to exist indefinitely so long as the subscribed capital remains in the enterprise, regardless of who owns the certificates. The Labour Share Certificates will have been issued to particular individual working partners and will be cancelled as soon as the particular worker leaves

[5] For a description of the many forms in which a Labour–Capital Partnership might be constructed see Meade, 1993b, pp. 107–126.

employment in the partnership. Share certificates will thus continue to earn dividends so long as the productive resource (the capital fund or the individual worker) continues to work for the partnership. The partnership would organise a pension scheme financed by contributions from the partnership, so that working partners on retirement would lose the dividends on Labour Share Certificates but would receive an appropriate partnership retirement pension.

Such a partnership will be of a discriminating kind. It will not be necessary to issue to an additional working partner more Labour Share Certificates than are needed to attract him or her to the partnership. In many cases this should make possible an expansion of employment which would be advantageous to all concerned. In many concerns it would probably be possible to find a range of rates of pay less than the rates of pay of the existing workers and low enough to make an expansion of employment profitable to the partnership as a whole, but simultaneously high enough to be very attractive to the unemployed worker. In such cases an expansion of employment would raise the incomes not only of previously unemployed workers but also of all existing partners, since it would produce a net profit which could finance an increased rate of dividend on all share certificates, whether worker or capitalist.

Where it was a matter of replacing a retiring member there would also be an incentive to find a new worker partner who could be attracted to the business by an appreciably lower rate of pay than the retiring member. Any saving of cost would increase the profit of the business and enable the rate of dividend to be raised on all share certificates, whether owned by worker or capitalist. This would be to the advantage of all concerned. All the remaining existing worker partners would gain by their share in the partnership's increased profit and the new worker would receive a higher income than he or she enjoyed in unemployment. The process of replacing a retiring worker partner by a less expensive worker would cause a shift in the income of the partnership from labour income to profit. The gain on each occasion would be divided between rewards on both types of share according to the number of each type of certificate. The number of Capital Share Certificates would be unaffected by the replacement of one worker by another worker, while the number of Labour Share Certificates would fall as a cheaper worker partner replaced a more expensive retiring worker partner. This would constitute a tendency towards a shift of income from wages to profits.

If these two processes of taking on cheaper worker partners for all extensions of employment and for all replacements of retiring members were adopted wherever possible throughout the economy, we could ultimately reach a situation in which the rate of pay was uniform throughout the economy at a level low enough to enable all jobs to be undertaken which produced a net revenue which was appreciably above the rate of unemployment benefit.

The paradoxical conclusion should be noted that any increase in output and employment at the expense of a reduction in the rate of pay will have been achieved by a series of independent decisions in the various partnerships, each of which will have been advantageous to all the individuals concerned at the time of each decision.

A widespread replacement of ordinary capitalist companies by Discriminating Labour–Capital Partnerships might thus greatly help to make acceptable any necessary reductions of labour costs in individual businesses. But it would leave unaffected the need for state action to offset the general undesirable redistributive effects of the relatively low real wage rates needed to maintain Full Employment. The political acceptability of any scheme which kept wage rates low in the interests of Full Employment will require some offset to these undesirable distribution effects, and such an offset requires the provision of some source of income other than wage payments. The discussion of these distribution problems in the following chapter will include proposals for decreasing the existing inequality in the ownership of wealth, so that the typical worker receives some income from property to supplement the payment for work, and for the payment to all citizens of an unconditional social benefit (called a Citizen's Income) to provide another source of income unrelated to pay for work done.

If there were such an unconditional social benefit it would be reasonable to reduce the level of unemployment benefit by the deduction of the unemployed worker's Citizen's Income. This would greatly increase the effectiveness of the Discriminating Labour–Capital Partnership by reducing the income which an unemployed person would lose by taking employment. This would in turn serve to reduce the rate of pay which a partnership would need to offer to the previously unemployed worker partners. This would tend to reduce the economy's real wage rate and thus further increase the levels of production and employment.

It would, of course, be totally unrealistic to assume that all businesses could take the form of Discriminating Labour–Capital Partnerships. But an actual limited shift in the direction of business structures based on the principles of the Discriminating Labour–Capital Partnership would help ease the political process of moving toward Full Employment.

Chapter 4

▲

The Distribution of Income and Wealth

In the last chapter we argued that the achievement and maintenance of Full Employment (in the sense of an unemployment percentage as low as 2 or 3 per cent) would almost certainly involve severe restraint on rates of pay in order to prevent a runaway inflation. We enumerated but did not discuss the policy instruments which had been tried or discussed in the past for such restraint over incomes and prices and added one institutional arrangement (namely the replacement of Capitalist Companies by Discriminating Labour–Capital Partnerships) which might help to make wage restraint more acceptable.

But that would certainly not cope with the basic problem. Rates of pay low enough to maintain the unemployment percentage as low as 2 or 3 per cent in a free-enterprise market economy would probably lead to an unacceptably low distribution of income as between earned and unearned income such as profits. Radical changes in fiscal arrangements will probably be needed to obtain a substantial rise in the incomes of those at the bottom of the distribution of the national income without raising their earned income above the relatively low level needed to maintain Full Employment.

There is one glaring absurdity in our present arrangements. The employers' and the employees' National Insurance Contributions are compulsory levies which constitute taxes on the employment of labour. For a Full-Employment policy, which threatens to have unfavourable effects on the distribution between earned and unearned income, to impose a special tax on the demand for labour (the employer's National Insurance Contribution) and another special tax on the wages earned by workers (the employee's National Insurance Contribution) marks the height of folly. These taxes should be abolished and the revenue replaced by more appropriate forms of tax, such as the income tax which falls on all types of income.

Any adjustment of income tax rates should as far as possible take the form of increased rates on very high incomes. The phenomenon of relatively low general rates of pay (even if they were relieved of the existing special taxes on them) combined with the excessively high rates of pay of the most highly qualified industrial specialists and, above all, of the managers of very profitable major industrial concerns – rates of pay of this kind being often in fact determined by the managers themselves – needs correction. A practicable correction could take the form of greater progression in the general income tax, the rate of tax on the highest slices of incomes being raised to 60 per cent or more.

Another suitable source for raising revenue would be a widespread charge or levy on all forms of pollution. The term 'pollution' is used to represent all cases in which the social environmental costs of certain activities are not being reflected in the private costs and prices at which such activities are being marketed (what the economist would call 'external diseconomies'). Such activities are the pollution of the atmosphere through the burning of fossil fuel; the congestion of road space through its free use for traffic and for the parking of vehicles; the disposal of wastes in rivers; the use of fertilisers which indirectly affect water supplies; the excessive use of natural resources; and so on. These problems should be tackled wherever possible by charging the polluter for the previously free use of the atmosphere or natural resources.

This can be done by the application of three rules: (i) to reduce the pollution by a tax or other charge rather than by direct regulation which raises no revenue; (ii) to tax the polluter rather than subsidise the non-polluting alternative (e.g., to tax the private car rather than subsidise the public bus as a means of reducing road congestion); and (iii) in those cases in which quantitative regulation is deemed to be necessary, to raise revenue by auctioning the necessary pollution permits to the highest bidder, rather than distributing the permits without charge on some other principle.[6]

The yield of revenue raised in this way could be very good. Not all this gross yield would represent a net gain, since the pollution taxation of some activities would lead to a reduction in the yield of other taxes on those activities. Moreover, in order to avoid the most undesirable distributional effects, the level of social benefits (such as the Citizen's Income discussed below) would have to be raised to offset the tax effects on the beneficiaries' cost of living. However, there would remain a very substantial net revenue bonus even after allowing for these offsets. The reliance on a pollution tax (whose incentive effects are socially desirable) rather than on taxes such as the income tax (whose disincentive effects on work and enterprise are undesirable) would enable a given level of social welfare to be maintained at a markedly lower social cost.

Another radical change which should be considered as an offset to the distributional difficulties of a Full-Employment policy is the payment to every citizen of a tax-free social benefit (to be referred to as a Citizen's Income) the level of payment varying solely according to the ages of the citizens, as children, or adults of working age, or persons of pensionable age. This would involve a

---

[6] See Appendix A at the end of this chapter for a modification of the second of these three rules.

hideously large budgetary expense which would be relieved (i) partially by the abolition of all personal tax allowances or reliefs under the income tax; (ii) partially by an offsetting reduction in such other social-welfare benefits as the citizen would have received in the absence of the Citizen's Income and (iii) partially by a withdrawal surcharge on the first *low* slices of all other earned or unearned incomes.

This withdrawal surcharge is a form of levy which in effect withdraws part of the Citizen's Income as a citizen's other income increases, a levy which is additional to the ordinary current rate of tax on income. This turns the Citizen's Income into something which is half way between a fully conditional social benefit and a fully unconditional one. With a fully conditional benefit a citizen without other income is given a full-scale benefit, but the benefit is reduced pound for pound as the citizen's other income increases. This is the cheapest way to ensure that everyone has a minimum guaranteed income. Benefit is paid only in so far as it is needed to bring income up to the minimum level. But it has the well-known effect of removing any incentive to earn any additional income, so long as any such income will be matched by an equivalent reduction in social benefit. On the other hand, a completely unconditional social benefit removes this disincentive effect, since the same tax-free social benefit is received regardless of the level of other income. But it is hideously expensive, in that it hands out free of tax an adequate social benefit to every citizen however rich or poor. The Citizen's Income with a surcharge on the first slice of other income falls between these two extremes. Every citizen, rich or poor, receives the same tax-free Citizen's Income but the surcharge on the first slice of other income is the equivalent of a withdrawal of part of the Citizen's Income, not pound for pound but, say, two pounds for every three pounds earned. The surcharge may, however, enormously reduce the cost of the Citizen's Income.

If this withdrawal surcharge is levied on a range of other income sufficient to repay the whole of the original Citizen's Income and if at the same time all forms of personal allowances on other income are removed, the total effect of the arrangement will be a very great redistribution of personal incomes obtained at a manageable fiscal cost. Richer citizens whose other income is greater than the range over which the withdrawal surcharge is levied will gain nothing from receiving the tax-free Citizen's Income. An equivalent amount will have been lost by the levy of the withdrawal surcharge and the loss of the personal tax-free allowance on the first slice of otherwise taxable income. At the same time, every citizen whose other income is sufficiently low to be within the range of income which is still liable to the withdrawal surcharge will receive the whole of the tax-free Citizen's Income plus a certain percentage of his or her other taxable income plus the excess of any special social benefit (e.g., disability benefit) over the Citizen's Income.[7]

A main objective of a Citizen's Income is to provide a reliable income from some source other than earned income (thus making the rate of pay less important relative to other sources of income) and to do so in a way which makes the personal distribution of the total national income more egalitarian.

Another approach towards this objective would be a change in fiscal policy which had the effect of reducing the present huge inequalities in the ownership of wealth. Unearned income in the form of dividends, rents, interest etc. on various forms of capital assets provides a reliable income which (like a Citizen's Income) does not depend upon the owner's rate of pay. Thus a more equal distribution of wealth (like a Citizen's Income) reduces personal inequalities in the citizens' total incomes. Such a redistribution in the ownership of wealth might be promoted by a combination of two reforms of our present tax arrangements.

In the first place, the existing general income tax would be transformed into a general expenditure tax by assessing

---

[7] For example, if the basic rate of income tax were 33⅓ per cent and the withdrawal surcharge were another 33⅓ per cent, the poorer citizen would receive the whole of the tax-free Citizen's Income plus ⅓ of his or her other taxable income. See Appendix B at the end of this chapter for a diagrammatic representation of this situation.

a citizen's income in the general manner in which it is at present assessed, but adding to this income all sales of assets and deducting from it all new purchases of capital assets. This constitutes a general tax on consumption expenditure since spendable income less net expenditures on the purchase of net additions to capital assets is equal to the income which in the absence of any general tax would be available for expenditure on consumption of one kind or another. If this was the basis for a general tax, it may be called a Saving-Exempt Income Tax (SEIT). To turn the existing Income Tax (IT) into a Saving-Exempt Income Tax (SEIT) would make it easier and more attractive to poor citizens with small capital wealth to increase their net savings and thus to increase the rate of growth of their properties.

In the second place, the loss of revenue due to the exemption of savings would be replaced by higher rates of wealth taxes of one kind or another concentrated only on large properties. Such taxes might take the form of taxes on the transfers of large properties from one ownership to another (i.e., transfers in the form of gifts during a benefactor's life or in the form of bequests on his or her death). There might also be an annual wealth tax on the ownership of large properties. There would in all cases be a high personal tax-free allowance on all properties so that these wealth taxes would fall only on that slice of any individual's wealth which exceeded a high exemption limit.

It would seem probable that the exemption on the savings of citizens with small properties offset by high wealth taxes on very high properties would lead to a gradual shift towards a more equal personal distribution in the ownership of wealth. It is true that people with small properties may not increase their savings because savings are exempt from tax; they may use the reduction in their payment of tax on their existing savings in part or even in whole to increase their consumption expenditures. People with large properties may finance the extra tax on them in part or even in whole by reducing their consumption expenditures. What is sought is not taxes which are *levied on* wealth or saving but taxes which are *paid out of* wealth or savings.[8] This particular feature of different taxes calls for greater expert analysis. It would, however, seem probable that a system which made it easier for those with small properties to save and less easy for those with large properties to add to their properties would lead to some tendency to redistribute the personal ownership of properties more equally.

The scheme which we have just discussed assumes that one can find a form of taxation which is paid largely out of the holdings and transfer of wealth and the savings of citizens who own large properties of one kind or another and

[8] I thank Professor Hahn for stressing the importance of this distinction.

that the tax revenue so raised is used to promote the savings of those citizens who own little wealth. An alternative and perhaps more radical use of such revenue would be to use it to finance what may be called measures of Topsy Turvy Nationalisation rather to subsidise the savings of citizens who possess little capital wealth.

With the nationalisation schemes undertaken, for example, by the Labour Government in the UK after World War II, the state took over the ownership and the centralised management of steel, railways, electricity, coal etc. But the state paid full compensation to the previous owners which meant that the state did not receive for its own free use the profits of such concerns, since this was offset by the payment of interest on the National Debt issued to raise the compensation cost of the nationalisation schemes. Thus the state became the owner-manager but without the benefit of an increased income. With Topsy Turvy Nationalisation the state obtains the beneficial ownership of the income earned on certain capital assets without undertaking any responsibility for the management of the business concerns, which is left to the private market.

To achieve this result the government must raise sufficient revenue (including not only any new revenue raised by new forms of tax which are mainly paid out of the savings or the holdings and transfers of capital of the wealthy property owners but also including all the other revenue-raising policies already discussed in this chapter) and it must restrict current budgetary expenditures sufficiently to raise a surplus of total revenue over total expenditure in the budgetary balance. This budgetary surplus might be paid into a National Asset Commission which replaced the present National Debt Commission.

The National Asset Commissioners would be independent of the government but would be under an obligation to use the funds they received to redeem any existing National Debt or to invest, like any private rentier, in investment trust and other appropriate forms of private assets on the competitive private Stock Exchange, or similar appropriate private markets for capital assets. Thus the state's saving would be mingled with savings of the private sector, for investment in productive enterprises which would continue to be competitively managed as free-enterprise undertakings.

The National Asset Commission could thus build up its holding of capital assets at a compound rate of interest equal to the rate of yield in profits, rents, interest, etc. on the state's savings. This rate of yield would, of course, be the post-tax rate of yield on these assets since the state would lose the tax which it would have received on these assets if they had been left in private hands.

At any time that it thought fit, the government could reduce the rate of build-up of the assets held by the National Asset Commission by increasing its budgetary expenditures or decreasing its normal tax revenue and thus reducing the budgetary surplus which it was paying into the National Asset Commission. But as long as it reduced its budgetary surplus by less than the current net build-up of investment income by the National Asset Commissioners, the process of build-up would continue.

This process would, however, be subject to one condition. Its continuation would mean that the state was mopping up assets which would otherwise have remained in the private sector. The possibility of separating state management from state beneficial ownership could be maintained only so long as sufficient wealth remained in private ownership for there to remain a sufficiently large Stock Exchange or similar market relying on the competitive forces of privately owned capital funds. If such private capital markets became too small, the National Asset Commission would not be able to operate in them as a pure rentier without dominating them.

This operation of Topsy Turvy Nationalisation could in theory be carried out at one fell swoop by a single huge Capital Levy. But such a step would be out of the question except in a highly revolutionary political atmosphere. The use of the annual revenue raised by a moderate rate of taxes which were paid largely out of the saving from, or the holdings or transfers of, large private fortunes may be regarded as a form of small annual Capital Levy.

Appendix A

A Distinction between Underdeveloped and Overdeveloped Economies

The rule suggested on page 53, to tax the polluter rather than to subsidise the non-polluting competitive alternative, does not mean that there are no conditions in which subsidies on such activities would be appropriate.

Consider the contrast between what may be called a generally underdeveloped and a generally overdeveloped economy. The former being both underpopulated and underindustrialised can easily absorb some polluting activities (e.g., a little smoke), some growth of population (e.g., using up only a small amount of available fertile land) and some consumption of natural resources (e.g., without depleting stocks of replaceable natural resources such as fish and timber and without substantial inroads into stocks of irreplaceable resources such as coal and oil). However, as the generally underdeveloped economy grows the cost of pollution, overcrowding and depleting stocks of natural resources will become greater and greater.

But at the same time there will be another factor at work, namely a rise in output per unit of input of resources due to the phenomenon of increasing returns to scale. As the size of the workforce increases, output per head can be raised by greater and greater division of labour (i.e., of specialisation of individuals on different tasks). As output increases, the capacity of production of lumpy forms of capital equipment can be used more fully so that output per machine rises. However, as the scale of the economy increases the possibility of reducing costs by a further increase in scale is reduced, as all possible useful divisions of labour become exhausted and all forms of capital equipment can be used to full capacity.

Thus there comes a point in the general development of an economy when the dangers of pollution, congestion, and excess use of natural resources have so increased and the possible reductions in cost due to a further enlargement of the scale of operation have so decreased that further growth of the economy would cease to raise and would start to lower total social welfare. At this point the economy would cease to be generally underdeveloped and would start to be generally overdeveloped.

Regardless of whether the economy is generally underdeveloped or overdeveloped, it is a wise policy to raise revenue by forms of taxation which will discourage anti-social activities. But a fiscal distinction arises in the use of the revenue.

In the case of a generally underdeveloped economy, the tax disincentive of anti-social forms of production will in itself reduce the scale of total output and will to that extent raise costs per unit of output. In this case, to use the revenue to subsidise lines of production which compete with the anti-social forms of activity will serve a double purpose. It will encourage the scale of the less obnoxious activities and thus help to restore the scale of total economic activity and at the same time, by reducing the subsidised price of the less obnoxious activities relative to the taxed price of the obnoxious activities, it will help to discourage the use and output of the latter.

In the case of a generally overdeveloped economy the restraint of scale of total operations due to the tax restraint on the obnoxious activities will in itself serve the double purpose of reducing the evil effects of the obnoxious activities and of reducing the congestion and excess use of natural resources due to the over-expanded scale of total production. The fair distribution of a restrained total national income then becomes the dominant consideration for the use of the increased tax revenue.

For example, the finance of a universal Citizen's Income would help to equalise the distribution of income. Any disincentives to total output resulting from such a payment could be more easily tolerated when the level of total economic activity threatened congestion, the excess use of natural resources and the pollution of the environment.

The analysis in this Appendix applies only to economies which are *generally* overdeveloped or underdeveloped. There are many economies which are overdeveloped in certain respects and underdeveloped in others. In particular, there are many economies which are horribly over-developed in having an excessively large population (which is also growing at an intolerably high rate and thus increasing the evils of overpopulation) but are at the same time horribly underdeveloped in having little or no efficient capital equipment. In these cases the analysis of general overdevelopment or underdevelopment is totally irrelevant. Population restraint with growth of efficient capital equipment requires quite different treatment.

In the present book the UK is treated as an economy which is generally overdeveloped rather than underdeveloped.

Appendix B

A Diagrammatic Representation of a Citizen's Income Financed by a Withdrawal Surcharge

The diagram (Figure 1 on page 68) represents the situation of a single taxpayer. The taxpayer's income from all sources before receipt of the Citizen's Income or other social benefits and before payment of income tax (which we will call the taxpayer's Unadjusted Income) is measured along the horizontal axis AB). His or her income after payment of income tax and after receipt of Citizen's Income (which we will call his or her Adjusted Income) is measured along the vertical axis AC.

The first adjustment is the payment of a tax-free Citizen's Income equal to AD; this tax-free boost to spendable income is payable to the taxpayer however great his or her Unadjusted Income.

The second adjustment is the imposition of a Basic Rate of income tax of 33⅓ per cent on all Unadjusted Income, without any personal tax-free allowance.

The third adjustment is the imposition of a Withdrawal Surcharge of 33⅓ per cent on all Unadjusted Incomes below a level equal to twice the level of the Citizen's Income (i.e., below AE).

The fourth adjustment is the imposition of a Surtax of

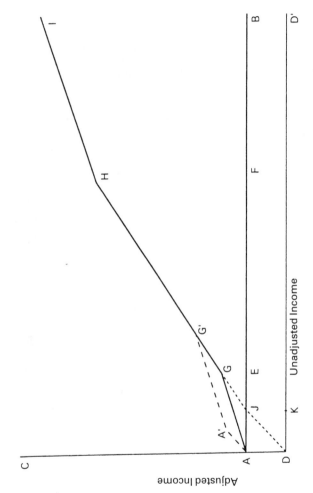

Figure 1 Citizen's Income with Withdrawal Surcharge and Surtax

33⅓ per cent on all Unadjusted Incomes greater than seven times the level of the Citizen's Income (i.e., greater than AF).

With these four adjustments, as the Unadjusted Income of the individual citizen rises, his or her Adjusted Income will be measured by the height of the line AGHI above the base line DD'.

Thus, over a first slice of Unadjusted Income equal to AE, the citizen will receive in addition to the tax-free Citizen's Income (DA) an amount equal to ⅓ of AE after a combined tax of ⅔ of AE, made up by the Basic Rate of tax of 33⅓ per cent plus the Withdrawal Surcharge rate of 33⅓ per cent on AE. Thus his or her Adjusted Income will rise along the line AG whose height is equal to the Citizen's Income of DA plus ⅓ of his or her Unadjusted Income AE.

Over the next range of Unadjusted Income EF, only the Basic Rate of tax of 33⅓ per cent will be deducted, so that ⅔ of any increase of Unadjusted Income in this range will be added to the citizens's Adjusted Income, which is represented by the upward slope of 2 in 3 of the line GH.

Over all Unadjusted Income higher than AF, a Surtax of 33⅓ per cent will be added to the Basic Rate of tax of 33⅓ per cent, so that the slope of the line HI will be reduced to 1 in 3, just as it was reduced to 1 in 3 by the Withdrawal Surcharge over the lower range of Unadjusted Income AE.

The result is a wide intermediate range of income subject to a Basic Rate tax of 33⅓ per cent, with the highest incomes constrained by a gently sloping ceiling and the lowest incomes supported by a gently sloping floor.

It is interesting to contrast the line AG with the dotted line DJG which represents the difference which would be made if one abolished the Citizen's Income and the Withdrawal Surcharge and reverted to a distribution in which the Citizen's Income was replaced by a personal tax allowance of an equal amount. Having abolished the Citizen's Income we must now take the point D rather than the point A as the origin of Unadjusted Income. With a personal tax allowance equal to the former Citizen's Income, the Basic Rate of tax of 33⅓ per cent will be charged only on Unadjusted Income higher than DK (= DA).

Over this first range of Unadjusted Income there would be no difference between Unadjusted and Adjusted Income, so that the dotted line DJ would rise at a slope of 1 in 1. But from the point J the dotted line would rise at a slope of 2 in 3 as only ⅓ of Unadjusted Income would need to be surrendered in Basic Rate of tax of 33⅓ per cent.

The result is that all citizens with Unadjusted Incomes to the right of the point G (i.e., on the lines GHI) would in fact be unaffected by a change from the personal-tax allowance regime to the Citizen's Income–Withdrawal Surcharge regime. But all poorer citizens to the left of the point G would have their spendable incomes raised by the difference between the height of the line AG over the dotted line DJG. Over the first tax-free range, Adjusted Incomes would rise from zero along the dotted line DJ at a slope of 1 in 1 and then along the line JGH at a slope of 2 in 3.

Thus the extra strain on the government's Budget due to the introduction of a Citizen's Income–Withdrawal Surcharge regime could be measured by the cost of the reliefs of poverty within the area AGJD, to the extent that it was not already relieved by the various existing social benefits. The result would be a great simplification and improvement of welfare benefits at the bottom end of the income scale.

In the simple form presented in this diagram it would, however, subject the Inland Revenue authorities to the difficult task of levying tax on all Unadjusted Incomes however low they might be. But it would be possible, if necessary, to allow some element of personal tax allowance on the lowest incomes. The dashed line AA′G′ shows the effect on the system of allowing a full tax-free allowance on Unadjusted Incomes below one half of the level of the Citizen's Income. Thus on these very low incomes, an individual citizen would receive the Citizen's Income plus a tax-free personal allowance on this limited range of Unadjusted Income. The citizen's Adjusted Income would thus rise at a slope of 1 in 1 on the dashed line AA′ over a range equal to half of AJ. The Withdrawal Surcharge of 33⅓ per cent plus the Basic Rate of tax of 33⅓ per cent would then restrict the growth of the citizen's Adjusted Income to a slope equal to 1 in 3 over the dashed line A'G'. The revenue cost to the budget would be increased by any problems of poverty within the area AA'G'G which were not already relieved by existing social benefits.

The incentive to seek work for citizens with extremely low incomes would be increased by the absence of any tax on such extremely low earnings; but for the somewhat higher earnings the range for a combined levy of 66⅔ per cent (Basic Rate plus Surcharge) would be extended from the point G to the point G'.

Chapter 5

▲

External Relations

So far this book has dealt exclusively with the problems of a closed economy. It has made no attempt to consider the far-reaching and very important implications of the proposed reforms for the international relations with other national economies. The present chapter will merely sketch some of the most significant features of the problems which would need close study and research if one country alone decided to introduce some of the basic elements in the proposed set of reforms.

The problems for the UK would be greatly reduced insofar as the governments of the member countries of the European Union, led by Germany, were to adopt similar appropriate sets of institutions and reforms. There would, however, remain merit in a certain degree of free experimental diversity in national policies. Some extensive recasting of modern free enterprise capitalist economic structures is manifestly required, but no one can say with certainty what precisely would be the best form for such recasting to take.

In any case, a widespread wholesale simultaneous adoption of the proposed domestic reforms by all major free-enterprise capitalist economies is clearly not a practicable proposition. The question remains how far and by what means a separate reform of one nation's economic policies in the direction proposed in this paper could in fact be made.

We may start by asking what would happen if the UK adopted the proposed domestic reforms while domestic arrangements remained unchanged in the rest of the world and in particular in the other members of the European Union. Any exceptionally low level at which real wage rates were held in the interests of Full Employment in the UK would, at current foreign exchange rates, cause UK products and services to compete heavily with the products and services of other countries both at home and abroad. UK exports would probably greatly increase and UK imports decrease, with a consequent improvement in the UK's balance of payments on current account.

In these conditions, if the UK wished to peg its foreign exchange rate at the pre-existing level, it would have to relax its monetary policy and reduce its rate of interest to balance the increase in its earnings of foreign exchange on current account with a matching decrease in its foreign borrowing on capital account. As a result of this the UK would in fact acquire part of the increased market for its products which was needed to maintain domestic Full

Employment at the expense of the market for foreign products and so for the employment of labour in other foreign countries.

This so-called 'social dumping' would be greatly resented by other countries on two possible grounds.

First, there might be general regulations against paying less in wage rates than certain minimum levels. Insofar as these were designed to defend the standards of living of the workers themselves there would be nothing in this criticism. The workers' standard of living certainly includes any tax-free Citizen's Income which is expressly paid to lead to a greater equalisation of standards of living. The UK would have to make sure that any Social Charter to which it was liable insisted on minimum standards of living for workers and not merely on minimum wage rates.

Second, and much more basic, other countries would resent very strongly the undercutting of their markets by products whose low price was maintained by what they would regard as wage costs held at exceptionally low levels by government intervention. In fact there would be nothing unfair in this element of so-called 'social dumping'. Provided there were no direct subsidisation of wage rates, the low real wage in the UK would represent simply what in a competitive market the wage would be if it adjusted itself so as to absorb the whole of the available supply of labour on the market. The presence of the tax-free Citizen's Income payable to every citizen, just like progression in an

Income Tax system, would be being made simply to improve the distribution of income. In terms of competitive market economies the fault would lie with the other countries, who by one means or another regulated the market price of labour at a level which restricted the demand for labour below the Full-Employment level. Let those other countries also reform *their* institutions on the proposed lines.

In fact, however, in present international political conditions it would be impossible to remain indifferent to the cries of unfair 'social dumping'. The UK would have at least to agree to adapt this low-wage policy in such a way as to expand its domestic demand solely for its own domestic products and not for foreign products, as a means of achieving Full Employment. The adverse effect on other countries could be met by the maintenance of higher interest rates than would otherwise be the case in the UK; and this, by diminishing the outflow and increasing the inflow of capital funds, would cause an appreciation of its currency which would make its products more expensive relative to foreign products and would thus eliminate any improvement of its current balance of payments which was due to the low wage costs and extra competitiveness of its tradeable goods and services.

But to rely exclusively on its monetary policy to control its foreign exchange rate at the level which would be needed to control its balance of payments on current account at the appropriate level would be disastrous for the implementation of the UK's domestic reforms. A basic feature of those reforms is to use monetary policy and so the rate of interest for two domestic purposes: first, to act as a short-term flexible instrument to maintain the UK's money GDP at its target level; and, second, to rely on its long-run level being low enough to maintain the long-run level of investment expenditures relatively to consumption expenditures at a domestically appropriate level. It could take no part in these two objectives if it had to be used to control the rate of foreign exchange.

Some compromise solution might perhaps be found in an agreement with the European Union's appropriate monetary authority on the following lines:

(1) an agreement on the rate of the peg of the pound to the European currency system which it would be appropriate for the UK to adopt in order to offset the effect of its low-wage policies on its international competitiveness;
(2) an agreement on a wide margin of permissible fluctuation above or below this agreed rate of peg; and
(3) an agreement for an annual review of the target rate of exchange set under (1).

The UK would aim at maintaining a substantial reserve of foreign currencies and this, together with the monetary agreement with the European Union under (1) to (3) above would provide a certain degree of freedom in the UK's use of monetary policies for its domestic objectives. But the freedom would still probably be inadequate for any really effective development of the whole range of domestic reforms suggested in this paper.

Greater freedom could be sought only by the use of fiscal policy instruments for the control of flows of capital funds into or out of the United Kingdom. If the practical administrative difficulties could be overcome, this might be achieved by (i) discouraging the outflow of capital funds from the UK through the imposition of a tax on the incomes of UK residents which arose directly or indirectly from the yield on capital funds invested anywhere abroad and/or by (ii) encouraging the inflow of European capital funds through the payment of a subsidy on the incomes of European residents which arose directly or indirectly from the yield on capital funds invested in the UK. These rates of tax and of subsidy might be adjusted so that, subject to the maintenance of an adequate reserve of foreign currencies, the expenditure under (ii) was covered by the revenue under (i).

Chapter 6

▲

Conclusions

The proposals discussed in the preceding chapters are obviously not to be treated as proposals for immediate application to the UK economy. Quite apart from the problem of their immediate political unacceptability, on purely economic grounds they could not be applied as a single total package of policies for three very different reasons.

In the first place, the many various monetary, fiscal and price-setting elements in the total package have been discussed only on general principles, without any quantitative assessment of the strengths of their effects. A great deal of econometric and statistical work would need to be done before a practicable package could be devised.

In the second place, the transformation of an economy with mass unemployment, threatened by inflation, with an extremely inequitable distribution of income and wealth, and deficient in skills and modern capital capacity into a Full-Employment, non-inflationary, fair and efficient economy could be achieved only over a considerable period of time by a continuing process of small changes in the various controls over the economy. These changes would be difficult in the early stages, when wage rates and consumption expenditures would need to be severely restrained. As the process continued and employment was increased, government tax revenues would rise and government expenditures on unemployment would fall; relief to the government budget would enable the proposed economic reforms to be carried out more and more quickly.

In the third place, the package of policies proposed in this book are based on a much simplified macroeconomic model of *some* of the main relationships between *some* of the main macroeconomic variables. Many other matters, including many non-economic considerations, would have to be taken into account.

It is clear from these three considerations that the exact package of reforms suggested in this book as being necessary to achieve and maintain Full Employment is, as it were, an unrealistic dream from fairyland. But does this mean that it is an intolerable waste of time to have written and to ask others to read it? Possibly not, for the following reasons.

The macroeconomic arrangements which are discussed here are in fact very important in the real world but are sadly neglected in the present discussions of Full-Employment policies.

The numerous reforms presented in this book's greatly simplified model of the economy constitute a package of changes which is devised for the limited purpose of dealing with only four basic economic desiderata, namely, acceptable levels of employment, of inflation, of the division of resources between investment and consumption, and of the personal distribution of income and wealth. The achievement and the maintenance of these four desiderata even in the greatly simplified model of this book involve no less than 21 control variables, namely:

(1) the current target level and future profile of the money GDP;

(2) the Central Bank's short-term money rate of interest;

(3) the choice between a tax on income or a tax on expenditure (SEIT) for the main direct tax;

(4) the level of, and the rate of progression in, the main direct tax;

(5) the level and the range of a withdrawal surcharge;

(6) the absence or the level of a personal allowance in the main direct tax;

(7) the level and personal allowance of an annual wealth tax;

(8) the level, personal allowance, and subsequent progression of a capital transfer tax (including transfers on death);

(9) the level of a tax-free Citizen's Income;

(10) the possible use of the Citizen's Income as a short-term demand-management control;

(11) the level of governmental expenditures on conditional social benefits;

(12) the level of governmental expenditures on domestic products of goods and services;

(13) to (20) the armoury of the eight forms of control over money prices and wages enumerated on pages 40–1 in Chapter 3; and

(21) the formation of Labour–Capital Partnerships.

The use made in this book of this formidable array of control variables and of institutional changes may serve to illustrate the complexity of the network of macroeconomic controls which would be encountered in the real world and to suggest some of the issues which would have to be faced in the real world.

The clashes of interest which would be encountered in finding an acceptable economic package of controls are also illustrated in a limited form in the present book – for example, the possible desirable effect of an increase in private investment on the use of resources for investment and its possible simultaneous undesirable effect on inflation. But there are many other cases of economic clashes which would have to be faced in devising a complete economic package for the real world. All the matters set aside in Chapter 1 would have to be taken into account.

Finally, it must be remembered that there is a whole range of social desiderata which must be considered in the formation of a package of economic controls. The final report of the Borrie Commission on Social Justice (1994) shows how wide is this range and how important in society are these social desiderata. The economic issues will play a large part, but not necessarily the dominant part, in the final choice of a total package of economic and social reforms.

The role of this book as a contribution to the final outcome is the limited one of drawing attention to the sadly neglected, but important and complex, macroeconomic factors to be taken into account in devising an acceptable Full-Employment policy.

References and Suggested Further Reading

Atkinson, A. B. (1993) *Beveridge, the National Minimum and its Future in a European Context*, STICERD Discussion Paper WSP:85, London School of Economics

Commission on Social Justice (Borrie Commission) (1994) *Social Justice: Strategies for National Renewal*, London, Vintage Books

Meade, J. E. (1993a) *Fifteen Propositions: concerning the building of an Equitable Full-Employment Non-Inflationary, Free-Enterprise Economy*, London, Employment Policy Institute

Meade, J. E. (1993b) *Liberty, Equality and Efficiency*, London, Macmillan

Meade, J. E. (1994) *Full Employment without Inflation*, London, Employment Policy Institute and Social Market Foundation

Parker, H. (1989) *Instead of the Dole: an enquiry into the integration of the tax and benefit systems*, London, Routledge

Simpson, D. (1994) *The End of Macroeconomics?* London, Institute of Economic Affairs

Index